Memories of Childhood

MARGARET WILLES

The National Trust

First published in 1997 by National Trust (Enterprises) Ltd
36 Queen Anne's Gate, London SW1H 9AS

© 1997 The National Trust
Registered Charity No. 205846
ISBN 0 7078 0228 8

A catalogue record for this book is available from the British Library

Text and picture research by Margaret Willes, Publisher, The National Trust

Designed by Peter Guy

Production by Bob Towell

Printed and bound in Hong Kong
Mandarin Offset Limited

Front cover: Toys and games belonging to Simon IV and Philip III Yorke at Erddig, Clwyd, now displayed in a reconstruction of their nursery. In the foreground is the toy train made by William Gittins, the estate carpenter, for Simon's fifth birthday in 1908.
Frontispiece: Rocking-horse head from the nursery at Attingham Park, Shropshire.
Back cover: Detail of the Day Nursery at Wightwick Manor, West Midlands, showing toys and books. Charles Voysey's design, The House that Jack Built, has been used on the curtains.

Introduction

When I visit National Trust houses, I often think about what it might have been like to have been brought up there – not only for the children of the master and mistress of the house, but also for the children of those who served there. In this booklet I have tried to evoke some of their memories, though only in the most recent years do we get reminiscences, and often they are written with tongue firmly in cheek.

The history of childhood is fraught with complications. Experts argue as to what this concept actually meant in earlier centuries. Parental love was clearly as strong then as it is now, and the lack of it just as upsetting, but the evidence that comes through is that boys and girls were expected to put away childish things much more quickly than they do now. In every area that I investigated, a change of attitude came about in Victorian times in families that could afford the luxury of allowing their children the leisure of childhood.

Most of the examples given in this book come from great country houses, as that is the area in which the National Trust is richly resourced. Particularly good examples of late Victorian nurseries can be seen at Lanhydrock in Cornwall and Wightwick Manor in the West Midlands. In other houses, such as Erddig, Clwyd, the nurseries have been reconstructed. There are also reconstructions of nurseries and a schoolroom at the Museum of Childhood at Sudbury Hall in Derbyshire, along with a fascinating collection of dolls, toys and games. For those wishing to see how the other half lived in the early nineteenth century, the Apprentice House at Quarry Bank Mill in Cheshire provides much food for thought.

Some of the material for this book has been drawn from Alison Honey's text for the 1994 Heritage Diary, and I am very grateful to her. Suzanne Whitehead at Sudbury has helped me with the toys and games, the spreads on children's clothes are drawn from Jane Ashelford's *Art of Dress*, published by the National Trust, and information about books has been inspired by Iona and Robert Opie's *Treasures of Childhood*, published by Pavilion Books.

CHILDHOOD as we know it passed as quickly as an April shower for many in earlier centuries. Few concessions were made: children shared the same clothes and books as adults and were encouraged to assume adult roles as soon as possible. Arabella Stuart took on her adult role at birth through her blood line. Her grandmothers were a formidable pair: Elizabeth, Countess of Shrewsbury, known as Bess of Hardwick, a lady of strong ambitions; and Margaret, Countess of Lennox, claimant to the English throne through her descent from Henry VII. These two played a dangerous game when they connived at the marriage of Bess's daughter to Margaret's son, resulting in the birth of Arabella in 1575, for Elizabeth I would brook no rivals to her crown. Lady Lennox spent a winter in the Tower of London, while Lady Shrewsbury was subjected to one of the Queen's terrifying tirades.

Despite the Queen's extreme displeasure, Bess seems to have clung to her dynastic ambitions. When she built the New Hall at Hardwick in Derbyshire in the 1590s, the state apartments were clearly designed to accommodate the royal visits of a future Queen Arabella. But this was not to be, and the pretty child shown in the portrait grew into a difficult and arrogant girl. Like Mary Queen of Scots before her, she became the focus of intrigues, kidnap conspiracies and secret marriage matches, and eventually died imprisoned in the Tower of London in 1615, a sad and slightly mad figure.

Elizabeth Percy's childhood was also blighted through her family connections, who engineered a series of dynastic marriages – all before she was fourteen. Her father, Joscelyn, llth Earl of Northumberland, died in 1670 leaving her, aged three, sole heir to his vast estates, including Petworth in Sussex. She was married at twelve to Henry Cavendish, heir to the Duke of Newcastle, but he died a year later. At thirteen she married Thomas Thynne but he was murdered in Pall Mall by her Swedish lover, Count von Königsmarck. A mere three months after that, she married yet again. Her third husband, Charles Seymour, 6th Duke of Somerset, immediately fathered a male heir, used Elizabeth's inheritance to remodel Petworth, and outlived her by 26 years.

Arabella Stuart, grand-daughter of Bess of Hardwick who commissioned this portrait in 1577 when the little girl was nearly two years old. She is shown holding a fashion doll (p.36).

L o s t childhood was not the prerogative of the rich and famous. For poorer families, adult responsibilities came quickly: as soon as children could walk they were put out to work, and girls often took on the role of mother to their younger siblings if their own mother died or was absent at work.

Some idea of the lifestyle of poor children can be gleaned from a visit to Quarry Bank Mill in Cheshire. When Samuel Greg established his cotton mill in a secluded valley of the River Bollin in 1783, he soon found that the villagers of the agricultural community at Styal could not and would not take easily to the regular hours and discipline of a large-scale factory. Instead he looked to the workhouses of Liverpool and Manchester, and even those as far away as London, to find his pauper orphan labourers.

These worker children were accommodated in a specially built Apprentice House close by the mill. By 1800 there were 90 child apprentices: 60 girls and 30 boys. They had been dispatched by their poor-law overseers with a set of clothes and a premium of two guineas for the cottonmaster. At the Apprentice House they were looked after by a superintendent and a medical officer ensured they were fit for work (p.12). Once accepted, they were fed, clothed, lodged and paid a penny a week for doing menial jobs in the mill. Older children were trained up, and some became skilled workers, but most were let go at the end of their seven-year apprenticeship.

One child described their food in 1806: 'Sundays we had for dinner boiled pork and potatoes, we also had peas, beans, turnips and cabbage in their season'. This sustaining diet was vital as they worked twelve hours each day, six days a week, with only Sundays free for church and schooling. In their precious spare time boys chopped wood and tended the vegetable garden, while the girls sewed sheets and did the laundry. At the end of the day, after this exhausting regime, they fell asleep – two to a bed.

A detail of the girls' dormitory in the Apprentice House at Quarry Bank, showing one of the beds that the girls shared sleeping top-to-tail, and the baskets where they kept their clothes.

WITH the nineteenth century came a new attitude towards childhood and children. Instead of being regarded as little adults almost as soon as they were able to walk, children found themselves encased in a world of their own – children, that is, of families that could afford such a luxury.

This change of attitude came about partly through the writings of the influential thinkers John Locke and Jean-Jacques Rousseau, whose views had a profound effect on the way people thought about the upbringing and education of children. Another factor was the picture of family life idealised by Queen Victoria and Prince Albert.

Where parents were loving and close, a Victorian childhood must have been wonderfully secure. The Robartes family of Lanhydrock in Cornwall are an excellent example. When Lanhydrock was badly damaged by fire in 1881, Thomas, 2nd Baron Robartes, commissioned the architect Richard Coad to build him 'a modest and unpretentious' home for his growing family. Visitors may be surprised by this description of Lanhydrock – to modern eyes it is far from modest. The accommodation for the Robartes children was placed on the first floor of a courtyard to the side of the main body of the house, and all the rooms faced south to catch the maximum light. Here nine children were brought up with all the facilities that money could provide. From the well-planned nursery, the children progressed to the schoolroom and a life filled with amateur theatricals, fancy dress parties and cricket teas.

The Fairfax-Lucys of Charlecote Park, Warwickshire have a very different story. Ada, eldest daughter of Henry Spencer Lucy, was badgered into marriage in 1892 to Henry Ramsay-Fairfax to settle the future of the estate. Both hated Charlecote, and their five surviving children were brought up in an isolated, loveless environment, their happiest times being spent with the servants. Sir Brian Fairfax-Lucy was so affected by his childhood that he collaborated with Philippa Pearce and wrote a fictional account that is now an established classic – *The Children of Charlecote*.

The eldest children of Thomas, 2nd Baron Robartes, in a group portrait painted in 1885 by Anna Lea Merrit. Thomas, the boy on the left, wears a kind of cavalier suit (p.32), while his twin sister Eva, on the right, has the fashionable decorative detail of smocking on her dress (p.30).

BEFORE the days of reliable contraception, it was quite common for women to be in a state of almost continuous pregnancy. This was particularly so amongst the upper classes where the custom of farming out babies to wet nurses meant that women didn't get the benefit of breastfeeding – one of the most effective means of natural contraception. Lady Elizabeth Brownlow, grandmother of 'Young' Sir John Brownlow, who built Belton House in Lincolnshire, bore nineteen children between 1626 and 1648, but only six of them survived infancy.

Childbirth was a hazardous experience for mother as well as child. Perhaps the most famous nineteenth-century case – with far-reaching consequences – was the death in childbirth in 1817 of Princess Charlotte, only child of the Prince Regent. She and her husband, Leopold of Saxe-Coburg, lived at Claremont in Surrey for the eighteen months of their brief marriage. A popular couple, they carried the hopes of a nation fed up with the quarrels of the Prince and the Princess of Wales, Caroline of Brunswick, and the bad behaviour of George III's other sons. After a traumatic labour of 52 hours, the 21-year-old princess gave birth to a still-born son: she died of a haemorrhage and shock the following morning.

The entire country went into mourning. Some examples of the memorabilia produced at the time can be seen at Croft Castle in Herefordshire. This house was, in fact, intimately connected with the tragedy, for Sir Richard Croft, the accoucheur who attended Princess Charlotte, was so depressed by his failure to save mother and child that he shot himself three months later.

Queen Victoria referred to pregnancy and childbirth as the *Schattenseite*, or shadow side, of marriage, although she appears to have sailed through nine births without miscarriage, infant death or danger to herself. She was delighted by the introduction of chloroform as a painkiller, and used it during the birth of her eighth child, Leopold, in 1853, describing the effect as 'soothing, quieting & delightful beyond measure'.

Princess Charlotte's death in childbirth is commemorated in this extraordinary painting of 1829 by an unknown artist, now hanging at Wimpole Hall, Cambridgeshire. Apotheosis of the Royal Family depicts Britannia mourning the deceased members of George IV's family and their reunion in heaven.

EVEN when babies had been delivered safely, there was yet another hurdle to overcome: surviving infancy. London bills of mortality for 1765 show a 60 per cent death rate for children under two, and in 1851 only 50 per cent of babies were expected to reach their fifth birthday. Insanitary conditions and the rapid spread of disease were largely responsible for this – epidemics of illnesses like smallpox, measles and diphtheria could wipe out whole generations of a family.

Illness respected neither rank nor wealth. In her old age, Mary Elizabeth Lucy of Charlecote wrote an account of her life, and an abridged version, *Mistress of Charlecote*, was published by Alice, wife of Sir Brian Fairfax-Lucy (p.8). In a chapter entitled 'Dark Leaves in the Wreath' Mary Elizabeth expresses her anguish as a mother when her little son Herbert Almeric was taken ill with a fever at Easter 1839. Despite the best medical attention, 'he passed away with so calm and sweet a parting it scarcely seemed like death, and there he lay in his little bed, peaceful and lovely as if asleep in that room that I have lived to call the *fatal* or *death* room, since every child born in it I have lived to mourn the death of.'

To recover from their grief, Mary and George Hammond Lucy made a tour of the Continent, taking with them their five surviving children including Edmund, born seventeen days after Herbert's death. As they crossed the Alps, Edmund was convulsed with a bowel complaint and died in the chaise. When Mary Elizabeth returned to Charlecote, she recorded: 'Home Sweet Home. There is no place half so dear to me, but my eyes did not remain dry when I thought of the deaths of two most dear and lovely boys.'

At Styal Mill, the medical officer, Dr Holland, looked after the pauper children for forty years. Some of his remedies can be seen at the Apprentice House, including leeches for bleeding and relieving fever. The most common ailment was inflamed eyes caused by the cotton dust in the mill, but Dr Holland also had to contend with accidents, such as that of Thomas Priestly, who lost a forefinger after catching his hand in machinery.

Herbs, remedies and recipes – but not the leeches – that Dr Holland would have used to look after the apprentices at Styal.

I N 1497 the Venetian Envoy to the Court of Henry VII recorded in considerable bemusement:

> The want of affection in the English is strongly manifested towards their children; for after having kept them at home till they arrive at the age of seven or nine years at the utmost, they put them out, both males and females, to hard service in the houses of other people, binding them generally for another seven or nine years ... during that time they perform all the most menial offices; and few are born who are exempted from this fate.

He refers to the custom of 'placing out' whereby parents paid other families of a similar social rank to take on their children as apprentices – to learn manners and perform household duties. Bess of Hardwick started her life in this way, in service in the neighbouring Derbyshire household of Sir John and Lady Zouche of Codnor Castle. Robert Barlow was also serving there in a like capacity: he became the first of Bess's four husbands in 1543.

In later centuries this detached attitude evolved into the habit of bundling well-born offspring into the realm first of nannies and nursemaids, then of governesses and tutors. The character of Nanny could have an enormous impact on her charges. Winston Churchill was devoted to his, Mrs Elizabeth Ann Everest, who supplied him with the unconditional support and affection that his socialite parents could not provide. By contrast, George Curzon drew a very short straw in the nanny stakes with Miss Paraman. After Curzon's death in 1925, handwritten notes recalling his suffering at her hands were found at the family home, Kedleston Hall in Derbyshire: 'In her savage moments she was a brutal and vindictive tyrant. . . . She persecuted and beat us in the most cruel way and established over us a system of terrorism so complete that not one of us ever mustered up the courage to walk upstairs and tell our mother or father.'

Jean-Simeon Chardin's painting of La Gouvernante now hanging at Tatton Park in Cheshire. Despite the title, the lady depicted is more like a nanny, commending to her young charge the serious aspects of childhood represented by the books tucked under his arm as opposed to the racquet, shuttlecock and cards, symbols of carefree play.

[14]

ALTHOUGH we think of country-house nurseries as established elements of the household, they were, in fact, comparatively recent additions, enjoying their heyday in Victorian and Edwardian times. Until the closing decades of the eighteenth century, most of the information we have about furnishings for child members of the household is gleaned from contemporary inventories and paintings, giving a tantalising patchwork of individual items rather than an overall view.

Records show wealthy families hanging children's beds with luxurious textiles, including silk, velvet and gold or silver cloth, oblivious to the practical details of damage and cleaning. The main nursery of Belton House is described in a late seventeenth-century inventory as being furnished with two four-poster beds, one with hangings of crimson mohair, the other curtained in grey angora. The 'little nurserie' meanwhile had a bedstead with purple curtains and a cradle complete with feather mattress and pillows.

Most cradles were made of plain wood, but a particularly elaborate example can be seen in William Hogarth's early eighteenth-century portrait of Gerard Anne Edwards. The baby is shown sitting in a wicker cradle, draped with yards of quilted fabric. Two other essential items of early nursery furniture were the high chair and the baby-walker, a contraption on wheels that supported small children as they learned to take their first steps. Both high chairs and baby-walkers are often depicted in early family portraits.

As the concept of childhood became more accepted, so too was the practice of confining children to the realm of the nursery until they were judged ready for entrance into adult society. Up to the mid-nineteenth century nurseries were usually situated as far away as possible from the social hub of the household: often this meant the attic.

Gerard Anne Edwards in his cradle, a painting by William Hogarth now hanging at Upton House, Warwickshire. The child holds a doll which is in a miniature version of a baby-walker.

I N the mid-nineteenth century nurseries were often shifted to within easy reach of the mother's boudoir and bedroom. This may have been due to the influence of Queen Victoria and Prince Albert, who spent many more hours with their children than most contemporary parents. The Queen, for instance, complained that the Buckingham Palace nursery wing was 'literally a mile off' making impromptu visits logistically impossible. This fault was corrected at Osborne House, her residence on the Isle of Wight, where a family wing was designed so that the royal parents had only to climb one flight of stairs to see their children.

Other country-house owners soon followed suit, including the Robartes family. When Lanhydrock was rebuilt in 1882, the nursery on the first floor was made completely self-sufficient, but was nevertheless within easy reach of Lord and Lady Robartes' private rooms. Visitors to Lanhydrock can see the nursery wing restored to its original appearance with a complete suite of rooms – scullery, night and day nurseries, Nanny's bedroom, bathroom and spare nursery/schoolroom – linked to the servants' bedrooms above and the kitchen below by the female servants' stairs.

The children slept in the night nursery, advancing from cot to bed, and then moving on to bedrooms of their own when old enough. Victorian and Edwardian memoirs constantly refer to the night nursery visitations of glamorous parents in evening dress on their way to the theatre or a ball. Sometimes this was the only time that children saw their mothers and fathers.

It was usual for the nanny to sleep in the room with her charges, but at Lanhydrock Nanny Coad had a separate room of her own, leading out of the Night Nursery and conveniently near the comfortable fireside for 'seasons of illness'.

The Night Nursery at Lanhydrock showing the cots for the youngsters and beds for older children.

LANHYDROCK boasts a particularly elaborate nursery suite, but most Victorian family homes had, at the least, day and night nurseries. The day nursery was a multi-purpose room where the children played and took their meals, and where Nanny and her assistants might sit in the evenings once their charges had retired to bed.

Wightwick Manor in the West Midlands is an Arts & Crafts house with a combination of antique tapestries, oriental carpets and porcelain, with William Morris furniture and furnishings. The Day Nursery was originally decorated with William Morris 'Bower' wallpaper, but the present decorative scheme dates from the 1930s, when Sir Geoffrey Mander married his second wife, Rosalie. The sunny room, painted in greens and yellows, became home to their daughter, Anthea Mander Lahr, who recalled her childhood memories of the Day Nursery in the summer issue of the 1992 *National Trust Magazine*:

> There was only a wind-up gramophone (not much admired) which played nursery rhymes and my father's election songs, and a piped-in wireless extension, permanently tuned to the nine o'clock news. The family discarded people but not things, so toys accumulated and, like the furniture, some date back to the 1880s. These hand-me-downs (now antique) were stowed at the back of the cupboard to minimise humiliation.

In some houses nursery food was prepared by the still-room maid and served by a footman specifically assigned to the nursery. At Wightwick, however, the food came from the kitchen, as Anthea Mander Lahr again inimitably describes:

> frugal meals consisted of eggs, baked beans, cheese dreams, roes and creamed haddock (my favourite).... This diet I supplemented by making condensed-milk sandwiches on a deliciously plastic, new make-believe stove. Having to eat such monotonous meals, indifferently served, created chronic digestion problems for many in the family. No wonder so many of the children from these nurseries found drink more palatable and comforting.

The Day Nursery at Wightwick Manor with some of the toys and games enjoyed, or not, by the Mander children.

THE last decade of the nineteenth century witnessed the flowering of nursery art. Eager parents flocked to luxury stores such as Liberty, Heals and the Army & Navy, which had begun to stock tiles, wallpapers and all the other essentials for the well-equipped and fashionable nursery.

Walter Crane was one of the first artists to concentrate on nursery furnishings, designing specifically for wallpapers rather than simply selling the reproduction rights of existing book illustrations. Between 1875 and 1906, Jeffrey & Co. printed eight Crane-designed wallpapers – one of them an exclusive design for the Castle Howard nursery in Yorkshire. Charles Voysey's charming 1929 curtain design of *The House that Jack Built*, now hangs in the Day Nursery windows at Wightwick. Also at Wightwick are two designs by the sporting illustrator Cecil Aldin, which appear on the Night Nursery frieze as well as Ellen Houghton's 'Days of the Week' in the tiled fireplace surround.

Along with the craze for wallpapers came the fashion for decorated crockery for nursery teas. Children's china was, in fact, the forerunner of commemorative mugs for royal events and momentous national occasions. Small charges were urged to eat off plates marking anything from 'The Opening of the Thames Tunnel between Rotherhithe and Wapping' to the death of Sir Robert Peel. However, towards the end of the nineteenth century favourite nursery book characters began to appear on dishes and cups – the beginning of merchandising. Kate Greenaway's designs were among the first to be used, followed by Mabel Lucie Attwell's distinctive characters, and finally – still popular today – Beatrix Potter's creations, Peter Rabbit and Benjamin Bunny.

A corner of the Night Nursery at Wightwick showing Cecil Aldin's frieze depicting a hen with her chicks, and paintings of 'Noon' and 'Night'.

NOON

NIGHT

SWADDLING very young children to stop them moving about and being sinful was a universal practice until the early eighteenth century. The baby was dressed in a shirt or other small garment, and bandages were wound spirally the length of the body. Physical needs were catered for with a tail clout – the Tudor or Stuart version of a nappy. Lady Anne Clifford describes in her diary how her husband, Richard Sackville, Lord Dorset, gave her three of his shirts to make into clouts in December 1619.

On his head, a baby would wear a biggin. In an early seventeenth-century portrait of four of Sir Thomas Lucy of Charlecote's children, the youngest is shown in an armchair with a red blanket – possibly his bearing cloth, which would have been wrapped around him at his baptism – and a biggin worn over his tightly fitting coif.

At four or six weeks, swaddling was discarded and the baby clothed in a 'frock', a waisted garment down to the feet. False hanging-sleeves were attached to the armholes as leading strings, to steady the child as he made his first faltering steps. Boys and girls wore aprons over their gowns until they were six or seven (p.29), but a boy's gown would have a shaped bodice like a doublet, while girls' dresses began to follow fashion, as can be seen in the portraits of the Lucy children and of Arabella Stuart (p.5).

In *Thoughts concerning Education*, 1693, John Locke condemned swaddling as contravening man's natural right of freedom possessed from birth, and by the mid-eighteenth century swaddling was no longer either philosophically or medically advocated. As Theresa Parker of Saltram (p.44) sensibly pointed out, 'a child is no sooner born than it is bound up as firmly as an Egyptian mummy in folds of linen'. Locke's recommendation that babies should sleep bare-headed took longer to be accepted, and caps continued to be an essential component of the infant wardrobe.

Four of Sir Thomas Lucy's thirteen children in a portrait painted in 1619. The little girls wear bodices and skirts of white and gold brocade, and the child on the left holds a coral on a chain as well as her pet bird. Their brother has a biggin over his coif and an apron with a bib over his bodice.

SMALL boys and girls alike wore long frocks in Tudor and Stuart times, but once a boy had reached the age of six or seven, he was 'breeched' – which meant he adopted the same type of dress as an adult man. In 1679 Anne, Lady North, described the breeching of her six-year-old grandson, Frank:

> Never had any bride that was to be dressed upon her wedding night more hands about her, some the legs, and some the arms, the tailor buttoning, and others putting on the sword.... When he was quite dressed, he acted his part as well as any of them.... They are very fit, everything, and he looks taller and prettier than in the coats [petticoats].

Jean-Jacques Rousseau, like John Locke, advocated that the physical and social needs of children should be considered separately from those of adults. In *Emile*, published in 1762, he declared, 'Before the child is enslaved by our prejudices, his first wish is always to be free and comfortable. The plainest and most comfortable clothes, those which leave him most liberty, are what he always likes best.' This revolutionary idea soon gathered pace, and boys began to wear loose-fitting coats made from light-weight fabrics, with a shirt open at the neck underneath, echoing the country suit adopted by men of the same period. This style of natural clothing can be seen in Sir William Beechey's portrait of the sons of Sir Richard Croft, in which the eldest boy, Herbert, wears a coat, breeches and an unbuttoned waistcoat over his frilled shirt.

In the 1780s yet another new silhouette was devised for boys – the skeleton suit. The trousers were cut to come above the waist and fastened to the bottom of a short jacket with buttons. The jacket collar turned back to the shoulders, revealing a frilled shirt collar. In the Croft portrait Thomas is shown in a skeleton suit with a red jacket. An eminently practical garment, it was worn by boys of all ages until its demise in the 1840s.

The four sons of Sir Richard Croft of Croft Castle, painted by Beechey in 1803. Francis, aged three, wears a white dress and a lace-edged muslin cap trimmed with blue ribbon. Herbert's sad expression and isolated position in relation to his brothers may be due to the fact this is a posthumous portrait: he died in 1803 while a pupil at Westminster School.

J U S T as seventeenth- and early eighteenth-century boys exchanged the long skirts of their frocks and aprons for scaled-down versions of adult dress, so their sisters wore a version of their mother's clothes. In John Closterman's 1696 portrait of the family of John Taylor Brook, now at Beningbrough Hall, Yorkshire, one of the girls is wearing a loosely draped satin nightgown over a low-cut smock – just like the languorous beauties of Charles II's court depicted on canvas by Peter Lely.

Echoing their mothers' costumes meant that girls as young as two were wearing boned bodices. A group portrait of Thomas Hill and his family at Attingham Park, Shropshire, shows the little girls wearing boned bodices with tuckers – frills of muslin or lace edging the low neckline. The older girl has a gauze apron just like her mother. But the philosophers of the Enlightenment had their effect, and girls' fashions too became more practical and free, with the restrictive boned bodices and skirts being replaced first by frocks and sashes in the 1770s, then by the Regency period's muslin chemise dresses with their high waistlines.

In Victorian times ladies returned to fussier styles – dome-shaped skirts supported by stiffened petticoats, and low necklines that cut across the shoulders to pinion the arms to the body. Frills, lace and ruching were the order of the day. By the 1850s, small girls echoed their mother's crinolines, but the shortness of their skirts obliged them to wear long pantalettes – loose drawers with frills around the bottom of each leg – a style memorably captured by Sir John Tenniel in his drawings of Alice for Lewis Carroll's *Alice in Wonderland* (1865).

Detail from Charles Philips's al fresco conversation piece of the Hill family in 1730, showing how children's dress – and gestures – echoed those of their parents.

ONE of the National Trust's major costume collections is lodged at Killerton House in Devon. Originally assembled by the actress Paulise de Bush, it contains more than eight thousand items of dress, including a comprehensive range of children's clothes.

The white cotton dress from the Killerton Collection shown here once again reflects adult fashion, this time of the 1870s. Such a dress would have been *de rigueur* for smart children's tea parties. As Arnold Bennett commented bitterly in *The Old Wives' Tale* in 1931, 'Weeks of labour, thousands of cubic feet of gas, whole nights stolen from repose, eyesight and general health, will disappear into the manufacture of a single frock that accidental jam may ruin in ten seconds.'

Great must have been the relief when, influenced by the Aesthetic and Arts & Crafts movements, girls' dresses moved towards the simple and practical, though the colours favoured by these movements tended to be in muted tones – in the words of one commentator: 'cobewebby grey velvet with a tender bloom like cold gravy'. Smocking, previously the provenance of the agricultural worker, now appeared as a decorative detail on girls' dresses, combined with a soft, broad sash around the hips.

For older girls in the late Victorian and Edwardian periods, standard daytime costume was the pinafore dress and blouse (p.33). Although giving ample room for movement, this style still involved a great deal of elaborate buttoning and many undergarments were worn below the apparently simple ensemble. Viola Bankes, recalling her childhood at Kingston Lacy in Dorset at the beginning of this century, wrote:

> We always wore Jaeger combinations in soft creamy-grey wool . . . . they had short sleeves and came down to our knees. Under our petticoats we also wore cotton knickers made at home and long black stockings, like little nuns. . . . Our sleeves were fastened tightly by a strap with one button. At first our frocks and pinafore were white which was then thought a very hygienic colour for children, as it showed the dirt.

A white cotton piqué dress in the polonaise style fashionable in the 1870s. The bustle effect is created by an overskirt edged with pleated fabric, which is echoed in the trimming of the bodice and sleeves.

IN the nineteenth century boys were 'breeched' much earlier than in previous times. The transition from babyhood to boyhood came at the age of two, when skirts were exchanged for tunic-style dresses with matching trousers. At six or seven this ensemble was exchanged for knickerbockers coming just below the knee, worn with a matching jacket.

For privileged Victorian boys, childhood fashion very much resembled a fancy dress parade – miniature soldiers, cavaliers, Scots and sailors; the last two inspired by the enthusiasms of the Queen and Prince Albert. Their love affair with Scotland, bolstered by the popularity of Walter Scott's novels, filled the nursery wardrobe with tartans, kilts, and Tam o'Shanters. Not all were convinced. In *The Science of Dress*, 1885, Ada Ballin warned parents of the dangers of kilt-wearing for boys, quoting the example of a six-year-old who had not grown since the age of three as a result of revealing his knees to the world.

The sailor suit was launched in 1846 when the tailor for the Royal Navy made one for Albert Edward, Prince of Wales, later Edward VII. In winter the boys' suit, with its wide-legged trousers and front flap fastenings, was made from navy blue wool; in summer, from a stout white cotton with blue facings. Girls shared in the naval experience with pleated skirts.

The First World War had a decisive effect on children's clothes. The number of servants available to help put them on and take them off dwindled dramatically, and children's basic requirements were at last recognised. Romper suits came in for toddlers, straight cut, low-waisted dresses for girls, and for boys – finally throwing off their knickerbocker suits and stiff collars – jerseys and shirts with soft collars, worn with shorts or flannel trousers.

Early twentieth-century children's clothes from the Killerton Collection. The girl's black wool smocked dress from around 1905, would have been worn when the family was in mourning. It is worn under a plain white pinafore. The boy's woollen sailor suit was made c.1910 to fit a seven-year-old.

IN 1985, the National Trust's take-over of Calke Abbey in Derbyshire attracted great interest, for here was a house where time stood still. The reclusive Harpur Crewe family combined a passion for collecting with an aversion to throwing anything away. As a result an eighteenth-century state bed was discovered in its packing case, a Burckhardt Shudi harpsichord emerged from the stables, and in the schoolroom a treasure-trove of childhood playthings was unearthed, from the doll's house and rocking-horse to dozens of dolls wrapped up in drawers, sets of lead soldiers in mint condition, children's books and games, tin trams on a wooden track and twenty miniature chairs. They had all belonged to Sir Vauncey Harpur Crewe, who inherited Calke in 1886, and show the range of games, toys and books available to the children of a wealthy family in the later nineteenth century.

But step further back in time and the variety of playthings diminishes sharply. Many children had to make do with the tools of their work and had little time for play. For these boys and girls, playthings were home-made and improvised. The Betty Cadbury Collection at the Museum of Childhood in Sudbury has some fascinating examples: a claypipe turned into a doll with the base painted to represent the face; a snake made out of stamps threaded on a cord; a miniature chest of drawers from matchboxes; a set of doll's house furniture from corks, pins, cretonne and string. Blue Peter has nothing on this ingenuity.

For those who could afford to buy them, toys were mass-produced in Germany from the end of the Middle Ages, reaching Britain through shops in towns and travelling pedlars hawking their wares at country fairs. Dolls, whipping tops, hobby- and rocking-horses, and wheeled toys can all be seen in paintings of children. These toys often had a serious purpose: girls would learn their needlework skills by making clothes for their dolls and stitching samplers; boys could learn how to sit on horseback from playing on their rocking-horses. For the most privileged young men, the art of war might be developed with sets of model soldiers, while their sisters used their doll's houses to teach them the art of household management (p.38).

A set of Victorian toy soldiers and their tin box, part of the treasure hoard found in the schoolroom at Calke Abbey.

[34]

THE portrait of Arabella Stuart on p. 5 shows her clutching a doll dressed in a style that would have been in vogue at the Tudor court a few years earlier. This is probably a 'fashion' doll, a device used by tailors, and later by dressmakers, to show their clients the latest styles. At Sudbury Museum of Childhood there are two exquisite early eighteenth-century dolls with heads of gessoed wood and their features picked out in stitching. Originally these were almost certainly fashion dolls given to children once they had served their purpose.

In the late eighteenth century dolls with wax heads were manufactured in fairly large numbers, and as the porcelain industry developed, the use of Parian ware (white unglazed china), glazed china and bisque also spread. All were relatively delicate materials, so children were expected to treat them with great respect, often playing with them only on high days and holidays.

For more robust play, parents would make dolls out of all kinds of materials. At Sudbury one of the earliest dolls, or babies as they were called, dates from the early seventeenth century. Carved from an oak stump, it looks as if a furniture turner improvised it for his daughter. Rags, teaspoons, matchboxes, dried apples and clothes pegs were all called into play to make dolls that could then be dressed by the girls' own home-made garments.

Portraits show that children have always owned pets as companions. An exotic menagerie – parrot, finch, marmoset and puppy – is shown in the sixteenth-century painting of Lord Cobham and his family, which now hangs at Longleat House in Wiltshire. At the beginning of this century the nursery's live pets were joined by an inanimate companion that was to prove a winner. When in 1902 Theodore Roosevelt, President of the United States, was presented with a captured bear cub while out hunting, his refusal to shoot the defenceless animal became the subject of a political cartoon in the *Washington Post*. Spotting the cartoon, an enterprising New York shopkeeper, Morris Michtom, made a stuffed plush toy bear for sale in his store: the Teddy Bear, favourite companion of so many children, was born.

Late Victorian dolls in the Museum of Childhood at Sudbury Hall.

T H E highlight of the well-furnished Victorian nursery was a doll's house. These very ornate and expensive toys enjoyed a long tradition: the first recorded baby's house, as they were originally called, was made in 1557 for Prince Albert of Bavaria. It is described as a perfect representation in miniature of a princely house, its furniture and fittings supplied by a whole range of different craft guilds. Although Prince Albert's house does not survive, several others from sixteenth- and seventeenth-century Germany can still be seen. Their original purpose was instructional, to help princes – or more often young ladies – to learn through play how to manage their households.

The National Trust owns two of the earliest and finest English baby houses. The first, from the 1730s, belonged to Sarah Lethieullier who brought it to Uppark in Sussex on her marriage to Sir Matthew Fetherstonhaugh in 1747. The house is three stories high, built on a base resembling a row of stables. Its nine rooms show the domestic arrangements of the period, with a well-equipped kitchen in the basement and a dining room on the floor above. Every detail is minutely accurate, from the pictures individually painted in oils to the hall-marked silver. The other example is at Nostell Priory in Yorkshire, and was made for the children of Sir Rowland Winn and Susanna Henshaw, who married in 1729. Just like the real Nostell, the baby house was designed by the architect James Paine, and the furniture was probably by the great cabinet-maker, Thomas Chippendale. The dolls representing the family are made of wax, the servants of wood. On the top floor is a lying-in room for childbirth, which even includes a wet nurse.

The Servants' Hall at Wallington in Northumberland is now given over to a display of doll's houses, most of them Victorian. Dominating the room is Hammond House, a mansion of 36 rooms on three floors, populated by family and staff of 77 porcelain-faced dolls, and over two thousand items of furniture. This house, created in the 1880s for an unknown family, boasts all the modern conveniences of the time: electric light, a working lift, and running water in the single bathroom.

The spectacular doll's house at Uppark, with the arms of the Lethieullier family in the central pediment. The house was made for Sarah Lethieullier c.1735.

T H E concept of children's books is a relatively modern one, as printing a book in the fifteenth century was far too expensive and elaborate a process to provide entertainment for young people. An instruction manual for children, *The Babees Book of Manners*, published in 1475, gives practical advice, including how to eat at table: 'when your potage [soup] you shall be brought, clean your spoon properly, and in your dish leave not your spoon, I pray'.

Books designed for children's recreation began to appear in England in the late seventeenth century. The Opie Collection, now in the Bodleian Library, includes a copy of one of the earliest, printed in 1672: James Janeway's *A Token for Children, Part Two* (part one remains undiscovered). It helped to establish a new tradition of addressing the child through narrative, though a lugubrious one to our eyes, for it consists of a sequence of anecdotes about small children dying in a state of grace. This book continued in print right through to the 1830s.

Relief from the Reverend Janeway and his ilk was soon on its way. In 1697 *Histoires ou Contes du Temps Passée*, edited by Charles Perrault under the pseudonym of Ma Mère l'Oie (Mother Goose), was published in Paris. This famous book of fairy tales included 'Cinderella' and 'Little Red Riding Hood' and was translated into English in 1729. At the time it didn't take the world by storm – it was used as a French/English reader rather than for nursery entertainment.

The range of children's books widened in the eighteenth century under the combined stimulants of technical advances and clever publishers. Mary Cooper's *Tommy Thumb's Pretty Song Book*, the first English collection of nursery rhymes, brought playfulness to children's literature when it was published in 1744. John Newbery, nicknamed the 'Jack Whirler' by Dr Johnson for his bounce and energy, published the first magazine aimed at children, the *Lilliputian*, which ran in parts from 1752. The development of metal engraving and litho printing made it possible to produce illustrated books that could then be hand-coloured. Thomas Bewick, and, later, the political satirist George Cruikshank, were among the well-known artists that worked on children's books.

The History of Little Goody Two-Shoes *published by John Newbery in 1766. Newbery, a great self-publicist, boldly claims that the original engravings were by Michelangelo.*

Little Goody Two-Shoe

THE HISTORY OF
Little Goody Two-Shoes;
Otherwise called,
Mrs. MARGERY Two-Shoes.
WITH
The Means by which she acquired her
Learning and Wisdom, and in conse-
quence thereof her Estate; set forth
at large for the Benefit of those,

Who from a State of Rags and Care,
And having Shoes but half a Pair;
Their Fortune and their Fame would fix,
And gallop in a Coach and Six.

See the Original Manuscript in the *Vatican*
at *Rome*, and the Cuts by *Michael Angelo.*
Illustrated with the Comments of our
great modern Critics:

A New EDITION, Corrected.

LONDON:
Printed for J. NEWBERY, at the *Bible* and
Sun in St. *Paul's* Church-yard, 1766.
[Price Six-Pence.]

B U T the golden age of books for children came in Victorian times. 'Toy books' had traditional texts with a strong individual interpretation, and were illustrated with colour pictures from wood-engraved or litho blocks. Routledge started their New Sixpenny Toy Books in 1866 and produced over a hundred titles within twenty years. Their rivals, with the 'Aunt Louisa' series, were Frederick Warne — later to be Beatrix Potter's publishers. Some of the most visually attractive are the books by the Arts & Crafts artist Walter Crane (p.22), recounting such tales as 'This Little Pig went to Market' and 'Sing a Song of Sixpence'. But he did not have the market to himself: the American artist Randolph Caldecott published sixteen enormously successful titles between 1878 and 1886, including ballads such as 'John Gilpin'.

The idea of writing an adventure story specially for children was unknown to the eighteenth century. Stories that were later to be identified as children's classics — Daniel Defoe's *Robinson Crusoe* (1719) and Jonathan Swift's *Gulliver's Travels* (1728), for instance — were originally written for adult audiences. The switch to exotic adventure came in the nineteenth century with *The Swiss Family Robinson* by Johann Wyss (1814), but this euphoric experimentation was followed by a reaction of decorum, and only in the 1840s was progress resumed with Captain Marryat's historical adventure, *Children of the New Forest*.

In 1846 Edward Lear published his *Book of Nonsense*, illustrated with his own specially prepared pictures. This uninhibited fun was followed two years later by untrammelled horror with the translation from the German of Heinrich Hoffman's *Struwwelpeter*. Victorian children were evidently not put off by the horrid fate that awaited them if they misbehaved, for it has become one of the best-selling nursery titles of all time.

With these three strands of adventure, humour and terror, the tradition of children's classics was set and continues today, from Lewis Carroll through Beatrix Potter and Rudyard Kipling, to Roald Dahl and Dick King Smith.

One of Walter Crane's illustrations from his version of 'The Yellow Dwarf' published in the Routledge Toy Book series in 1875.

'MOTHERS must give up their boys but keep girls constantly under their eye,' was the declared view on education of Theresa Parker, the eighteenth-century mistress of Saltram House in Devon. Although in their early years boys and girls looked indistinguishable in their dress, once the day of breeching came at the age of four or five, the boundaries between the education of the sexes were firmly laid. To ensure the proper training of conduct and character of the privileged young, governesses were employed for girls, and boys were often prepared for entry to public schools by private tutors.

Tragically Theresa Parker was not able to put her views into practice: she died two months after giving birth to a girl, also named Theresa, leaving the infant and a three-year-old son, Jack, in the care of her husband John and her sister Anne. At the age of seven Jack was sent as a pupil to Dr Kyte's school in Hammersmith on the outskirts of London, over two hundred miles from Saltram. Anne wrote of the day he left for Hammersmith that 'He behaved at parting with his usual propriety, though I believe there was a shower [of tears] in the chaise.'

His younger sister, meanwhile, remained at Saltram to be instructed by a French governess in the schoolroom. Anne recorded Mademoiselle's arrival: 'I flatter myself we have got a treasure in her as Governess, she is perfectly good natured, well behave[d], modest and seems sensible.... Her not speaking English I look upon as her greatest advantage, as she has no temptation to mix with the other servants.'

Governesses and tutors often found themselves in this odd limbo-like position in the household – above the servants in social status, but definitely below the master and mistress of the house. Ursula Wyndham, who was brought up at Petworth in the early twentieth century, wrote in her autobiography *Astride the Wall* that governesses were 'totally isolated. Parents left them in sole command of the schoolroom and treated them with the distant civility they extended to the domestic staff. The governess was intent on proving her gentility but nobody was interested.'

Henrietta and George Harry Grey play while their governess reads. A charming portrait by Hugh Douglas Hamilton, 1767, at Dunham Massey in Cheshire.

FORMAL education was a blessing enjoyed by the children of the wealthy. Working-class families could rarely afford either the money required to attend school, or the time spent away from the fields or the factory. But philanthropists through the centuries have offered education for the poor: medieval cathedral schools; Reformation grammar schools; charity schools such as Westminster's Blewcoat School, founded in the early eighteenth century and now used as the National Trust's London shop. Sunday Schools provided basic literacy and numeracy for thousands of children from the 1780s, as did the British and Foreign Schools founded by the non-conformists, and the National Schools established by the Church of England in the early 1800s.

To some the very idea of educating the poor was a dangerous precedent. One MP in the early nineteenth century posed the question, 'What produced the French Revolution?' and gave the answer, 'Books'. But fortunately his view did not prevail. James Kay-Shuttleworth of Gawthorpe Hall in Lancashire, who became a leading educational administrator, declared that the state had the responsibility 'of rearing . . . children in religion and industry, and of imparting such an account of secular education as may fit them to discharge the duties of their station'. His vision was put into practice in 1870 with the passing of the Education Act, enabling local authorities to finance Board Schools from the rates.

Victorian schools were often run on the monitorial system, with teachers instructing the older pupils who would in turn pass the lessons on to the younger children. The actual schoolroom was usually oblong, with tiered seating so that the teacher could both see and be seen: reconstructions can be seen at Shugborough in Staffordshire and at the Museum of Childhood at Sudbury. But what cannot be reconstructed is the incredible noise that must have ensued – to avoid resonance, it was recommended that the schoolroom should have no ceiling and the floors should be of rammed clay. A world apart from the quiet gentility of the governess and her country-house schoolroom.

The Victorian Schoolroom at the Museum of Childhood, Sudbury, showing the desks laid out with writing slates and slate pencils. The abacus was used to teach arithmetic.

Household Management

Margaret Willes examines the tasks of the housekeeper, the nursery maids, the butler and the cook, focusing wherever possible on specific individuals – Mrs Garnett, the eighteenth-century housekeeper at Kedleston, Derbyshire, and Mrs Coad, who presided over the Victorian kitchens at Lanhydrock, Cornwall – to provide a fascinating insight into the lives of the men and women behind the daily organisation of Britain's country houses.

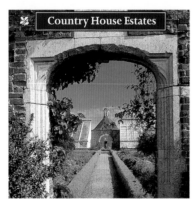

Country House Estates

This companion guide to *Household Management* investigates the out-buildings and their personnel – from the land agent and the laundrymaids to the gardener, gamekeeper and the stable lads. Once again Margaret Willes uses the anecdotal evidence of employers and their servants to bring the past to life in an exciting and vivid manner.

Care of Clothes

How did our ancestors care for their clothes – remove an accidental stain or the mud from a day in the fields? Jane Ashelford describes the innovative – if laborious – techniques developed over the centuries before science created crease-free fabrics and perfected dry-cleaning, and Shelley Tobin, curator of the National Trust's largest costume collection, recommends how to preserve and store precious clothes handed down through the family.

PHOTOGRAPHS

National Trust Photographic Library

The National Trust, front cover, p.27
Nadia MacKenzie, p.1, p.39
John Hammond, p.5, p.9, p.15, p.29
Keith Hewitt, p.7, p.13
Roy Fox, p.11
Angelo Hornak, p.17, p.45
Andreas von Einsiedel, p.19, p.21, p.23, p.31, p.33, p.37, p.47, back cover
Derrick E. Witty, p.25
Michael Freeman, p.35

The Publishers also wish to thank:
Bodleian Library, University of Oxford (Opie Collection), p.41, p.43

ISBN 0-7078-0228-8

£4.99

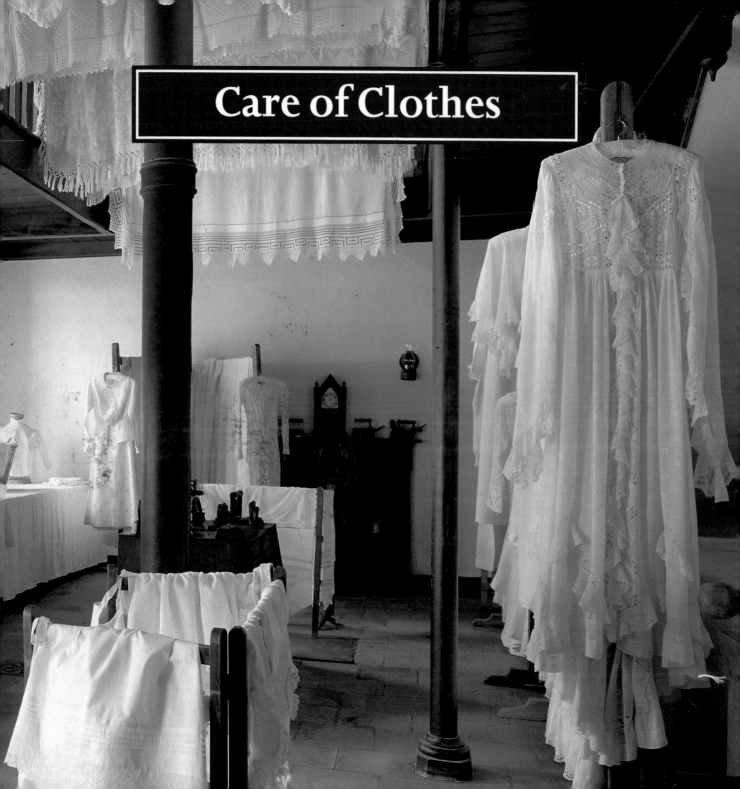

Care of Clothes